Table of Contents

Sermon 8
Lies and Faith 9
Chakras 10
Senryu ~ Ghosting 12
Senryu ~ Overload 13
Graveyards 14
The Crop Next Door 16
November 9, 2016 17
Gifts 19
Half-Staff 2022 21
He's Somebody's 24
Eintou ~ Say No 26
Harvest 27
Senryu ~ Quarantine 28
Kwansaba ~ She 29
What is Grief?? 30
Vases 32
Truth Hurts 33
Sandcastles 35
Senryu ~ Lessons 36
Silent Fuck You 37
Senryu ~ Let's Talk 38
Senryu ~ Edit, please 39

Invisible Pain	40
To Those Who Never Grew Up…	42
Deafening Scream	43
Roller Coasters	44
Cropped	45
Sijo ~ Autumn Leaves	46
Freedom Bloom	47
Plot Twist	48
I See Dead People	50
Pray	52
Fairly Wicked	53
Yes to Me	55

Tunnel Maze
Simply Sherri
©2023

All rights reserved. This book or parts thereof may not be reproduced in any form, stored in any retrieval system, or transmitted in any form by any means— electronic, mechanical, photocopy, recording, or otherwise—without prior written permission of the publisher, except as provided by United States of America copyright law. For permission requests, write to the author at simplypoeticentertainment@gmail.com

Acknowledgments

I must thank two poets for inspiring several poems in this collection. Rasheed Copeland, in October 2016, challenged himself and other poets to write poems in a new form every day. Dr. Rebecca Dupas creates writing prompts every October for a small group of poets.

Thank you, Analysis, for your hard work editing this collection. Alex Alexander, the cover design is better than I could have ever imagined.

To my family and friends who have stood by me during these dark years, I know I only made it through with you telling me to rest, letting me cry, and allowing me the space to retreat into a corner when I needed it.

Introduction

Tunnel (Noun)
    an underground passage.

Maze (Noun)
    a confusing network of intercommunicating paths or passages.

Tunnel Maze – Definition

A long depressive episode where there is nothing but darkness. Every light at the end of the tunnel turns out to be another wall.

I made this statement to a friend explaining my mental state at the time. I felt stuck on a path that I had no idea how I ended up on and could not escape. Every bit of progress I made towards a goal turned out to be a mirage, and I wound up being pushed ten steps back. I didn't notice the tunnel growing around me; I was going through life. Events kept happening, I kept dealing with them, and things just got darker and darker.

There were occasional flashes of light, bits of hope, but then a new wall would appear. Through it all, my friends and close family stood in my corner prepared to catch me when I fell apart, which didn't happen until my mother passed.

A friend came to me and said, "I've watched the light in your eyes dim," and here I thought I was hiding my condition.

As I compiled this collection, I started to see faint lights at the end of this labyrinth. The book contains poems about faith, politics, love, and mental health.

Hope you enjoy it.

Sermon

Psalm 30, verse 5
For his anger is but for a moment, his favor is for a lifetime.
Weeping may endure for the night, but joy comes in the morning.

We are not told how long the night will last
Not cautioned about the nightmares
The words do not protect us from the bogeyman

Remember, it's always darkest before the dawn

We are just asked to endure

To believe

Have faith

Eventually, there will be

Peace
Pleasure
Prosperity

Ultimately, there will be better days.

Lies and Faith

I believed every lie
I told myself about you
I dismissed every clue
I found to the contrary
I had no foundation for hope
Faith doesn't work that way

Chakras

He said my forehead was beautiful
And since that last word dripped off his lips
When so many can't see past my frame
I was left wondering
What was I thinking
What thought was floating on my brain waves
That made the space above my eyes
The most noticeable thing about me
Did his eyes see a royal color my aura was releasing
Or were my chakra vibrations
Controlling his third eye's vision
This felt so nice that I decided to stop

Analyzing
Rationalizing
And just start enjoying being in his presence

Let his serenity stream into my conscience
Quieting any questions, I may have about him
He asked me to follow him down a long road
If I didn't feel some obligation at home

For him
I would permanently change my zip code
No need to exchange names
No desire to play those cat-and-mouse games

As our time came to a close
He drew me into his arms so close
All my inhibitions became unfroze
I wanted to stay there in his arms so tight for the rest of the night

But being the lady that I am
This time I had to let go of this man

I still wonder...
What was I thinking
That made the space above my eyes the most noticeable thing
  about me

Senryu ~ Ghosting

Deciding to ghost
Is a relationship crime
Sentence: life, no me

Senryu ~ Overload

Moonlight in Cancer
Emotions on overload
Revisit later

Graveyards

I only visit graveyards
When it's time to commit my loved ones' remains to the earth
I drop flowers
Kiss the casket
Whisper my final goodbye
Walk away remembering how this person touched my life

I think one day I'll go and visit
Bring fresh flowers
Brush away debris
Speak to the granite headstone
They can hear me, right?

I just have to go to the gravesite
They would be with me
But I don't go to graveyards

There are no graveyards to visit for the relationships
I've watched die
Those I have shed a thousand tears over
The ones I denied were ending with attempts to resuscitate
I felt their heart stop beating for me
Yet I still tried

Two rescue breaths; count...

Push life
Pump the heart 30 times
Push the love again
2 Breaths
30 pumps again
2 Breaths
30 pumps

I'll keep doing CPR
Long after the time of death has been called

Now I'm supposed to drop the flowers
Kiss the casket
Watch it slowly descend into the crypt and walk away

I'll continue living in this graveyard
Periodically exhuming the corpses
Reperforming the autopsy
Searching for the cause of death
Searching for the clues I missed
Searching for some clarity so I don't do it again
Freeing all the ghosts so they don't haunt my next relationship

I don't visit graveyards but, in my mind,
I refuse to leave this field of headstones
This graveyard full of relationships
That have come and gone
Left me a little more broken
My search for forever is haunted by these ghosts
Of lost loves

I'm suffocating
Buried alive in the cemetery
But now that I'm seeing the error of my ways
I'm going to stay here for a little while longer
Start digging again
Searching for the relationship I just buried
The one I killed
Before it even had a chance to breath

The Crop Next Door

Social Media is a well-tended garden
Full of attractive photos
Happy couples
Romances in full bloom
Aspirational vignette

But

What's in the manure that nourishes it?
Was the soil weeded after previous harvests?
Is the lighting artificial or natural?
The crop next door is beautiful

But

Will what keeps it flourishing
Be deadly in another field?

November 9, 2016

I picked up the phone

Called my boss

I gotta call out today...

I call out
Black
Woman
Inconsolable

I call out...poet
My free speech is under attack

Yes, my throat hurts

I'm sick, angered, disgusted
This is so sad
I'm still trying to figure out what the fuck just happened

Can we call it Jury Duty
Present me the testimony
Where is the evidence
I need to pass judgement

I call out ally
I cannot stand back and witness this crime
My friends are being robbed of their rights

I call out middle class
Retirement just got farther away
To my desk I'll still be chained
Can I enjoy one more day before I start to feel enslaved

I call out unmarried
Black
Woman
The way this new world is now ordered
I feel a little less protected

Can I use a bereavement day?
I'm mourning the death of civility
Common sense

I need some extra time to pray for my ancestors, my decedents
This is a family emergency

I call out mother
Of daughters
Future sons-in-law
Be black men
One reservist
One day, I want to nuzzle fat grandbabies
Who will be their fathers when they have brightened the targets on
The backs of their men?

This is a mental health day
I need some time to order my steps
Figure out what's next
And convince myself
This nightmare won't be as bad as it's going to be

So boss, I gotta call out today

She told me "No
We need you to do what you do
To ensure it won't happen again
And to guarantee that this Black university survives"

Gifts

The worst relationships I have ever been in are with
men that do not listen
They refuse to pay attention

It really shows after they fuck up
And want to give me a gift

It's something that doesn't seem to be for me
It's not in my size
Nothing I would've asked for

In fact
I can almost tell that it was a last-minute purchase with how
haphazardly
And passively it was presented
And he expects thunderous applause just for giving it.

Right now, I'm in a relationship I can't seem to get out of

America, we did not need a holiday on Juneteenth

We didn't wish for capitalism to insert its tone deafness into it either

I pretty sure the wish list stated
Reparations
Anti-lynching legislation
Our voting rights to be protected
We just want you to leave us alone in our communities you are
Systematically shattering

Yet you keep giving us performances and
Ice cream and party supplies
Then lighting Yankee candles to cover the stench of racism
This new act is late

Like the holiday it's trying to commemorate.

Are we supposed to forget the massacres in our communities
When the victims were blamed

Rosewood, FL
Bogalusa, MS
Wilmington, NC

We keep presenting the receipts, but you refuse reimbursement

How many times will they destroy our living rooms before you acknowledge it?

But I guess I'm asking too much from people whose ancestors attended lynchings for entertainment.

This is not a holiday for everyone to celebrate
For some, it's a day for education, reflection and atonement

For the decedents of the enslaved, a holiday from white nonsense

America, this relationship could improve
If you would close your mouth
Open your eyes and ears, and
Make the real changes that we have been demanding

Half-Staff 2022

Outdoor concert
Nightclub
Movie theatre
Grocery store
Shopping mall
Office building
Military installation
Church
Mosque
Synagogue
College campus
High school
Middle school
Elementary school
One-room schoolhouse

They were all just going about their lives' business when…

The morning news opens with a picture of The White House
Silhouetted against the clear azure sky with the American flag
Flying at half-staff
A symbol of respect that has lost some of its meaning
When it's in that position for the fourth time in less than a year
Flying in the low posture to honor the civilian casualties outside of any active war zone

From the smallest of towns to the largest of cities
Communities of people living their lives
The massacres keep happening
The body count keeps rising
We keep asking what can be done…
Looking over the Capitol dome
They are flying the flag half-staff

They will say mental health issues are to blame,
Too many are desensitized by the violence in video games
They were a loner
We didn't know what they were planning
But the past few days they were acting kinda strange
We didn't know how to help—
Or didn't care enough to try

Next, the lobbyists will start expounding,
"It's our right to bear arms
Tougher purchase rules and background checks infringe on our freedoms"
But would it have mattered
Most perpetrators had not committed a crime before they start shooting
So, I'm back to asking
Why?
I'm asking: Do we really need access to military grade weapons?
Why is there a need for assault rifles for hunting ducks and deer in open fields?
Isn't it clear that the only prey being killed are humans in confined spaces?
At the Supreme Court
The flag is at half-staff

The families left behind deserve more than inaction
National mourning should not be persistent
The proper response is no mystery, isn't magic,
It doesn't require a Mystic
We need representatives that want to really make a difference

Because soon as all the shouting is over
All the finger-pointing done,
The politicians and pundits finished sending
their thoughts and prayers
What will we have?

A growing list of innocent victims
One more candlelight vigil
Another moment of silence
Next year another "remember when that happened" story
And the government doing exactly what they will agree that they are
empowered to do to prevent this from happening again

They will fly the flag at half-staff

One-room schoolhouse
Elementary School
Middle School
High School
College Campus
Synagogue
Mosque
Church
Military installation
Office Building
Shopping Mall
Grocery Store
Movie theatre
Nightclub
Outdoor Concert

They were all just going about their lives' business when...

He's Somebody's

We need to love each other out loud
This secret affection for men
This no-one-needs-to-know going on between us
Needs to come to an end

We owe it to the world
We have to show the world,
They need to know that when something happens to a black man
Any black man
He is loved
He is needed

He's that friend who's the shoulder you can cry on
He's a mentor who freely gives advice
He is his community
He's part of a story that only three to four people and God know
He's the guy whose sister's best friend's grandmother can call for anything

He's someone's favorite cousin
He's integral to
The family he was supporting
The mother who birthed him
The grandmother who's expecting him for Sunday dinner

He's not a threat
When he's playing by himself
He's not a threat
When he complies
He's not a threat
When he's standing doing business
He's not a threat
When he's walking minding his business

I'm not saying they are all angels
Or perfect pillars of the community
He's not the bad apple spoiling the bunch
His life has value
More than an instantaneous moment of fear can encapsulate

That man has a partner with whom he's making memories
His laugh is their favorite smile
Praying over him
Will cry for him
He's the love of someone's life
He's the twinkle in someone's eye
His heartbeat is someone's lullaby
He's the exasperated daddy answering 5000 questions
His disappearance will leave an unfillable hole

He's the love of someone's life
He belongs to somebody
He is needed
He is wanted
He is loved
He's somebody's

Eintou ~ Say No

Say no

Loudly, clearly roar NO

You are not doing that now

Your body is too young for this conversation

He wasn't a friend before then

He won't be later

Say no

About Eintou:

The Eintou is an African American poetry form consisting of seven lines with a total of 32 syllables or words. The term Eintou is West African for "pearl" as in pearls of wisdom, and often the Eintou imparts these pearls in heightened language.

(Reference https://poetscollective.org/poetryforms/eintou/)

Harvest

Praying
Toiling
Planning
Daily

Assessing
Revising
Weeding
Weekly

Waiting
Watching
Exercising
Patience

Harvesting

Joy
Peace
Love
Beauty

My arms are full

Senryu ~ Quarantine

Before protesting
The quarantine examine
Stance on women's rights

Kwansaba ~ She

Her smile widens while gazing at photos
Recalls stories of bumps, bruises, lost teeth
She feels the memory slip into corners
Fading into the shadows of her mind
She pauses at the newest image...smiles
Allows a single tear to escape happy
She will live on in their smiles

About Kwansaba

The kwansaba is a poetic form invented by Eugene B. Redmond in 1995. It was inspired by the seven-day holiday of Kwanzaa, including its seven principles of unity, self-determination, collective work, cooperative economics, purpose, creativity, and faith.

Reference
https://www.writersdigest.com/write-better-poetry/kwansaba-poetic-forms#:~:text=The%20kwansaba%20is%20a%20poetic,purpose%2C%20creativity%2C%20and%20faith.

What is Grief??

what is grief but love persevering ~ WandaVision

Grief develops like a tsunami
Formed on aftershocks
There's no warning
The tide does not pull away from the beach
The wave overtakes you
Praying the receding waters leave my memories

Grief produces avoidance
Including your extended family
Sitting in the corner in tears
You want to attend the celebration
But the last time we were together was the worst day of my life.

Grief scrambles your mind
The brain doesn't quite work the same
Attention is fleeting
Memory no longer exists
The inner voice is always asking questions
Is this healthy?
Is it avoidance?
Is it toxic positivity?
Is it just overthinking?
Can it please stop?

Grief is a DJ
Curating your playlist
The O'Jays were once on repeat
After my mother climbed the stairway to heaven
They could not be listened to

Grief is not a sprint or marathon
It's a hike through the Himalayas
Every breath gets harder
I hear there will be beautiful scenery along the way.

And whether or not I want to it's a journey I'm forced to take.

Vases

Caring for a loved one with dementia
Is watching a vase slowly fall from a shelf
And shatter.

Truth Hurts

We are told
Don't lie to your parents

The truth will set you free

But how do you tell the truth to someone whose memory won't retain it

How do tell my dad the love of his life has passed on
Again

Dementia is my dad regressing to a time before he knew me.
To the one we know from stories told by frat brothers
To the little boy we've seen in my grandfather's home movies

He asks, *where's your mother*
She's away with her sisters
Can you call her
Her phone is broken
Why hasn't she come to see me
I'm not sure; let me ask my sister

Eventually, he will change the subject

It's the web that must be spun
Conjuring answers to his questions
To keep him from feeling that hurt again

Mom, I'm sorry for spinning this web of deception
To keep him content
I can't take seeing him cry again

He asks: *What time is David coming by?*
Uncle David didn't tell me he was coming
Let's call and talk to him
Thankfully I don't have to lie this time

Sandcastles

After we experience forever,
Go by the ocean on the brightest day
Build me a sandcastle close to the water
Build it imperfect
With many layers
Let the tides inch closer and closer
When complete
Let the sea claim it

Don't watch
Remember the fun you had building it
Remember the fun we had building us
Then walk away
Think of it
And me
And smile

Senryu ~ Lessons

Revisit past loves
Research the lessons learned
Live the report

Silent Fuck You

When considering responding to a belligerent hater
please take the following advice

Never
Never
Underestimate the power of the eloquently delivered silent "fuck you"

Fuck the opinions
Fuck their feelings
Fuck the fact they are breathing

They are not worth your time or energy
Not worth turning your grey matter red thinking about 'em

Haters are going to hate
Attention whores will stunt for maximum reaction
Ignoring them requires no energy on your part
And still causes them pain

Cause: flesh-eating bacteria from the inside

Let them hold their breath
Force them to smile
While waiting for you to respond

Senryu ~ Let's Talk

Communication
Instantaneously solves
Life complication

Senryu ~ Edit, please

Sometimes a writer
Needs to take time to edit
Today's poem done

Invisible Pain

I wish he would have just hit me
I know what I'm saying may sound crazy
But I'm telling you some things in my life would be better
If maybe, he would have just hit me

Left me with black and blue wrists
Swollen eyes or with something that would have required stitches
Then I'd have proof that I've been hurting

But I'm not that lucky

My attackers have been more insidious
Thousands of small attacks
Eroding me at my foundation
Stripping away my confidence
Shredding what's left of my self-esteem
Leaving a shell of my former self
Just existing

Really, I wish he would have just hit me
Then I would have been able to scream
Cause a scene
Someone might have called the police
Then I'd have witnesses to my pain

But I'm not that lucky

These attacks are designed to keep my body whole
Free from blemishes and bruises
For him, they are of no use
All that's wanted is a broken soul
No thoughts of my own
Mind controlled
Not feeling safe at home

Words hitting harder than
Any fist that Tyson would throw

I wish he would have just hit me
Then jumping from a simple touch
Wouldn't seem so strange
My issues would be clear
Trust
Love
Intimacy
I would be believed
Visible disfigurement
Would be my testimony
Instead of wounds
Hidden behind bright eyes, counterfeit smiles

Now I know if he had hit me
Eventually, he may have killed me
But my physical death must be better than what
I have become accustomed to…

A spiritless existence

To Those Who Never Grew Up....

Neverland must be a beautiful prison.

Deafening Scream

Bluish-grey clouds are rolling in
Bright flashes signal the thunder in them
The silence is deafening

Fear-flavored tears stain my face to start a scene
I feel invisible hands tighten around my throat
I want to scream

Something wicked comes howling in the wind stream
Negativity, despair, anxiety mix with the voices
The silence is deafening

How long before I see the sun again
Touch happy, hold peace, breath in relief
I want to scream

I start to ask for assistance
No one is listening
The silence is deafening

When depression comes it's loud, demanding
The fight makes my voice a whisper
The silence is deafening
I still need to scream

Roller Coasters

I don't like roller coasters
Adrenaline-filled joy rides are not for me
I am afraid of heights
Hate that stomach-dropping feeling

The Rebel Yell
Incredible Hulk
Goliath
Steel Dragon
None of these names sound like anything I want to be on

I like my feet firmly planted on the ground
Hand me your wallet and keys
Go enjoy the ride
I'll watch you fly
Rejoice in the joy you found

In life
Whether we just cool
Or decided to do eternity together
Put me in the front seat next to you
Eyes wide open
I'll ride with you

I'm in the seat next to you
Through all the twists, turns
Ups downs upside downs
I promise to be here

Did I mention I hate roller coasters?
However, I will endure this life's ride for you.

Cropped

I grew the chain that held me bondage

Planted it
Nurtured it

THWAACK

Deep exhale

THWAACK

Back straightens

THWAACK

Chains break
Five minutes of effort

Released five years of coiled up tension
Chopping out
Heart breaks, job losses
Health issues anxiety issues
People I had to leave behind
Memories I was chained to
Holding myself hostage
Captive to the image that
I'm only beautiful with long hair
Gazing down the aftermath
Laying on the ground
I breathe easier
Now
I'm free

Sijo ~ Autumn Leaves

Autumn is a reminder

      that change is necessary, beautiful

Exfoliating thickening skin,

      shedding outdated beliefs

Revealing, exploring,

      Harvesting a new season of happiness

About Sijo:

A Sijo is Korean verse form comprised of three lines of 14-16 syllables each, for a total of 44-46 syllables. The form is related to Haiku and Tanka.

(Reference https://www.poetryfoundation.org/learn/glossary-terms/sijo)

Freedom Bloom

When nurtured
Protected

She blooms

Flaunts the fullness her beauty

She will feel safe
Untouchable

This is freedom

Plot Twist

I've seen enough movies to recognize a plot twist when I see one ...

Boy did we hit the fast forward button
Missed a few scenes
Skipped some character development
Strayed from the manuscript
Someone did improvisations
We were meant to be stunned by the plot twist
Who the hell saw that coming
It wasn't a *Fatal Attraction*
But still could be a *Titanic* mistake

We both had personalized copies of the script, right?
Nothing in these pages
Said anything about this
Being a fairy-tale-ending romantic comedy
Where two-star crossed lovers spend a lifetime
Searching for the love they think they have missed
It's a buddy flick...

Sorta *When Harry Met Sally* before New Year's Eve
Not to be extended into *9 1/2 weeks*
The stuff I'm reading is not award-nomination worthy
Kind of boring

Why would anyone want to see this film
An ongoing tale of misadventures
Meeting up in random places
Hands shaking…hugging occasionally
We'd tell stories over drinks
One or two random shared experiences
Then move on into the next take

When this happened, I was still trying to figure out

Why the last movie tanked
Especially when it all looked so good in the sheets
My pages said move on solo
Show the world who you are
Keep going

Yours were ordered steps
Arranging the scenery
Setting the table for
The Princess Bride
Whom you'd cherish forever (as you wish)

I was meant to be the comic foil
Just here to chew up scenery
Have another wonder
Why she's even here
She's just messing up the happy ending

This should not be a turning point
An event that extends the story for another sixty minutes
Attempting to script another ending
Will turn this into a *Nightmare on Elm Street*
There is no cliffhanger demanding a sequel
Even though the scene was really good
It can be left on the cutting room floor

Get the clapper
End scene
Roll credits
Story complete

No plot twist needed!

I See Dead People

I see dead people.
All the time.
They're everywhere.
Walking around like regular people. They don't see each other.
They only see what they want to see. They don't know they're dead.

They only see what they want to see. They don't know they're dead.

Even though appearing to be human and full of life
They are not engaged in what is going on around them
No inner being
They are just walking shadows of their former selves
The will to live has left them

I see dead people

Zombies caught up in the day-to-day
Carrying the weight of the world on their shoulders
Atlas would be proud; you do it with a smile
While
Drowning in self-doubt
Asphyxiating on unmet expectations
Cutting selves with blades of self-pity
Ingesting poisonous stress
Hanging ourselves by hanging onto what's letting us go
Life is not an AMC episode
Going through life like The Walking Dead
Was never meant to be living

They only see what they want to see; they don't know they are dead

Living with negativity
Don't even see the blessing in breathing
Wish it was understood the release that comes

When addressed
When written
When spoken
There is freedom
Cease committing suicide by feeding your inner demons
They feed off our swallowed tears

I see this most with poets

Yes, there is crying in spoken word
Stop apologizing for it
You wrote that for a reason
You never know who else needs to hear it
Let the words flow
Until you feel the weight has lifted
Help someone else through it
Get to the end of your suffering
Keep speaking your truth; it releases you

I'm tired of seeing dead people
They don't know they're dead
I don't need a Sixth Sense to see them because I used to be one

Pray

Sometimes it's just needed
Pray peace
Pray understanding
Pray love
Pray to ease stress
Pray breaking chains

Regardless of the language pray

Pray healing minds
Pray healing hearts
Pray healing the sick
Pray nightmares disappear
Pray cure

Regardless of the language pray

Pray equality
Pray good sense
Pray relief
Pray safe homes
Pray change

Regardless of the language, creed, religion, pray

Fairly Wicked

The difference between holding a magic wand or a broomstick

Environmental

Energy cannot be created or destroyed
It can only be changed in structure
Magic is energy

Depending on who is present magic is transformed
Prince Charming or Prince of Darkness
Glinda or Evilene

The difference between
Arriving on bubbles awash in bright light
Or in a cloud of green smoke

Chemistry

We try to control it
Keep down the turmoil
Mystically it still manifests
Some just bring our worst
Taking us out of the *Somewhere Over the Rainbow* peace we discovered
Creating a being acting heartless
This was never the aim

We just want to be magical
Create beauty wherever we go

Often our efforts are naught
Regardless of how many times we try chanting incantations of
Peace and harmony
It results in vengeance
We are only allotted finite amounts of glitter to shine

Why waste it on negativity
You can't pray to remove the
Stumbling block that you keep placing
Trying to change a bad situation
Screaming "Get thee behind me, Satan!"
When you invited him to entertain you

Some days the best you can do is smile sweetly,
Innocently, drop a house, turn around, find the road, ease on down…
Oz is out there and it ain't coming to you

Move away from the gift-giving small people
They believe they are well-meaning while reporting all the bad news
Attempting to stunt your growth
There is no time for this

Start the journey—if necessary, alone
Like-minded spirits will be found along the way
Making the trip more enjoyable

Assist you in fighting the
Flying monkeys that some crank sent to your door

We are magical
How we fly in with our wings
Or on the broomstick
Whether fair or wicked
It's all a reaction
To the energy in the room

Yes to Me

It's me
I'm the problem
I'm the one who has forgotten what yes to me sounds like

It sounds like

No, I'm not ok
Yes, I can use your help with this task
Yes, to treating myself better
Yes, to additional rest - TODAY
Yes, to my self-interest regardless of yours
No, that never made me selfish
No, I'm not going to be the bigger person or code switch right now

Yea I've always been beautiful
Yes, I'm open to a loving relationship
Yes, I'll wait for the bartender to finish making this drink
Yes, I'mma pay for it
No, I didn't wear this outfit for you
No, my looks didn't change because I no longer wish to engage in this conversation
No. Don't ask again

Yes, to making my own money
Hell yes, this is how I'm spending it
Yes, to immersing myself in things I love
Yes to joy
Hell yes to my pleasure
Yes to how I get there
No, that may not include anyone else

Yes, to how I honor the god I worship
Yes to making space for your life's religious practice
No to whatever bs you are trying to sell me as religion

Yes to spending time with my friends
Yes I'm open to hear what you need to talk about
Or no, right now might not be the best time; can I call you later?
Yes I'm always here for you
I just need to remember to be there for myself

Sometimes saying no to you is saying yes to me

And if I say "oh hell no"

Then yes you fucked with the wrong one.